THE BROADWAY Ingenue

39 THEATRE SONGS FOR SOPRANO

ISBN 978-0-634-08231-3

HAL•LEONARD®

Visit Hal Leonard Online at
www.halleonard.com

Contact us:
Hal Leonard
7777 West Bluemound Road
Milwaukee, WI 53213
Email: info@halleonard.com

In Europe, contact:
Hal Leonard Europe Limited
42 Wigmore Street
Marylebone, London, W1U 2RN
Email: info@halleonardeurope.com

In Australia, contact:
Hal Leonard Australia Pty. Ltd.
4 Lentara Court
Cheltenham, Victoria, 3192 Australia
Email: info@halleonard.com.au

FOREWORD

*A*n ingénue is broadly defined as a fairly innocent, pretty young woman. It is as common in theatre as any character type, with roots that go back to the Greeks. Such characters abound in Shakespeare. And the tradition is by no means over. Ingénue characters can be constantly spotted in movies and on television as well as in plays and musicals. On the musical stage such characters have roots in the soubrettes and romantic leads of opera, or in the leading female roles in French operettas by Offenbach, English operettas by Gilbert and Sullivan, in zarzuelas, or in Viennese operettas.

Some ingénue characters are static throughout a story, with no fundamental transformation. Others go through some struggle or crisis and evolve to more worldliness. Ingénues can be single or married young women. Some are quite serious by temperament; some are mischievous; others show a more comic or flirtatious side. Ingénues can be light characters who simply grace the story with their presence and charm, or they can be more complex young women who show deeper emotions. But they always retain an essentially lyrical, feminine quality.

In musical theatre traditions the ingénue is typically a soprano (although it does happen that ingénues are occasionally belters). This collection is a sampling of soprano songs from many ingénue roles. Among the most famous are Kim MacAfee in *Bye Bye Birdie*, Guenevere in *Camelot*, Julie Jordan in *Carousel*, the title character in *Cinderella*, Luisa in *The Fantasticks*, Sarah Brown in *Guys and Dolls*, Cosette in *Les Misérables*, Marion Paroo in *The Music Man*, Eliza Doolittle in *My Fair Lady*, Laurey in *Oklahoma!*, Christine Daaé in *The Phantom of the Opera*, Magnolia Ravenal in *Show Boat*, Maria (and Liesel too) in *The Sound of Music*, Maria in *West Side Story*, and Amalia in *She Loves Me*. In this revised edition contemporary ingénue songs have been added from *The Light in the Piazza*, *The Little Mermaid: The Broadway Musical*, *School of Rock* and *Little Women*.

There have been many well-known ingénue sopranos on Broadway and in movie musicals. To name a few: Julie Andrews, Barbara Cook, Shirley Jones, Jane Powell, Kathryn Grayson, Deanna Durbin, Rebecca Luker, Sarah Brightman, Kristin Chenoweth, and Kelli O'Hara.

Contrary to popular belief, portraying an ingénue is not necessarily easy on stage. It can be much easier as an actress to play a character with more edge, or more idiosyncrasies to hide behind. The eternal challenge is how to find an interesting way to play an ingénue, or sing such a character's song, so that the result is not standard-issue bland, but has some spark of life and individuality.

In other words, portraying an ingénue in song requires all the same creative imagination and investigation as any other acting assignment. Using her song as a guide, you must find her spirit and the details that make her unique.

Do you have an ingénue inside you, to breathe new life into these wonderful songs? You don't have to wonder "Wouldn't It Be Loverly." Just choose a song and begin to "Make Believe."

Richard Walters
editor

CONTENTS

* This song, recorded by Kristin Chenowith on *Let Yourself Go*, is not from a show.

ANOTHER SUITCASE
IN ANOTHER HALL
from *Evita*

Words by Tim Rice
Music by Andrew Lloyd Webber

*It would be stylistically appropriate for the pianist to improvise an accompaniment.

all the same I hate it, would - n't you? So what hap-pens now? So what hap-pens

now? Where am I go-ing to? _____ Where am I

go-ing to? _

Time and time a-gain I've said that I don't care; That I'm im-mune to gloom, that I'm

hard __ through and through: But ev-'ry time it mat-ters all my words de-sert me; So

an-y-one can hurt me and they do. So what hap-pens now? So what hap-pens

of this sad oc-ca-sion; But that's no con-so-la-tion, here and now. So what hap-pens

now? So what hap-pens now? Where am I

go-ing to? ___ Where am I go-ing to?___

THE BEAUTY IS
from *The Light in the Piazza*

Words and Music by
Adam Guettel

With a strong pulse

CLARA:

These are ver - y pop - u - lar in It - a - ly!

It's the land of na - ked mar - ble boys! ___

Some - thing we don't see a lot in Win - ston Sa - lem.

That's the land of cor - du - roys! ___

Poco più mosso, flowing, but exact tempo

I'm just a some-one in an

in It - a - ly. Ev - ery-one's a fa - ther or

a son. I think if I had a child

I would take such care of her. Then I would - n't

feel like one. I've

hard - ly met a sin - gle soul, but I am not a - lone._____ I feel

Tempo II (Poco più mosso)

known! This is want - ing some - thing. This is pray - ing for it.

This is hold - ing breath and keep - ing fin - gers crossed. This is count - ing bless - ings.

This is won - d'ring when I'll see that___ boy a - gain. ___

BEYOND MY WILDEST DREAMS

from Walt Disney's *The Little Mermaid – A Broadway Musical*

Music by Alan Menken
Lyrics by Glenn Slater

me here! Walk - ing a - round, strange as it seems, some - where be - yond my

wild - est dreams!

I'd hoped and wished and won - dered what I'd

do here. Wished and prayed and pic-tured what I'd see.

Prayed, and wow! My pray'rs are com-ing true here.

Look at it all, look how it gleams! Love-ly be-yond my wild-est

dreams. _____

THE GIRL IN 14G

Music by Jeanine Tesori
Lyrics by Dick Scanlan

Pets are banned, par-ties too, and no so-li-ci-

ta-tions. Win-dow seat with gar-den view.

No swing

A per-fect nook to read a book. I'm lost in my Jane Aus-ten when I

decresc. poco a poco

À la "Tristan" (no swing)

hear: "Ah, ah."

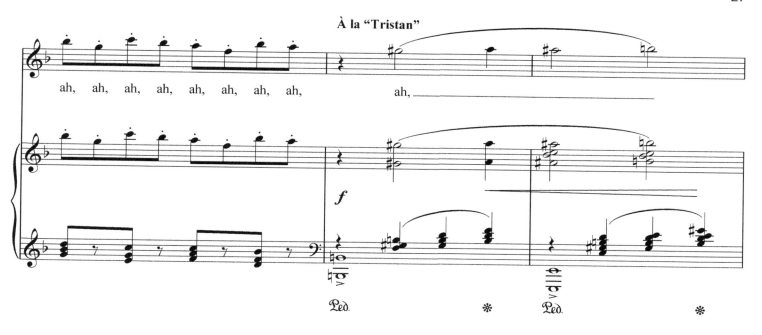

À la "Tristan"

ah, ah, ah, ah, ah, ah, ah, ah, ah,

À la "Magic Flute"

ah, ah, ah, ah, ah, ah, ah, ah, ah, ah, ah, ah, ah, ah, ah, ah, ah, ah,

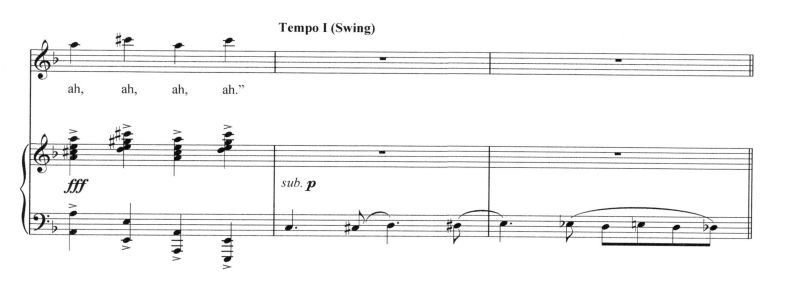

Tempo I (Swing)

ah, ah, ah, ah."

No swing

Now I lay ___ me down to sleep. ___ A com-fy bed

to rest my head. A stretch, a yawn; I'm al-most gone, then

Fast Jazz, à la Ella Fitzgerald (Swing)

"Doo - wee - zwah ___ doo -

tah - dup - doo spee-di-lee dee-floy-doy bee-blip, ___

naa - naa - naa - naa - naa - naa - naa - naa - naa - naa - naa - naa, woo - weeee.

Tempo I

Now the girl up - stairs wakes me un - a -

wares. Blow - in' down from Fif - teen "G" ___ her

rev - eil - le. ___ She's scat - tin' like her name is El - la. Guess who an - swers a cap - pel - la.

sub. **p**

mp
lightly

Broad swing

Ah." Had my fill of peace and qui - et. Shout out loud. I've changed my di - et, all be - cause of Four - teen "G!"

HERE AT HORACE GREEN
from *School of Rock*

Music by Andrew Lloyd Webber
Lyrics by Glenn Slater

ROSALIE:

Here at Hor-ace Green, our
At our hal-lowed school, the

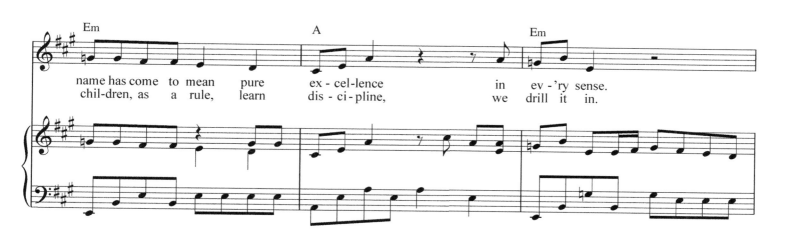

name has come to mean pure ex-cel-lence in ev-'ry sense.
chil-dren, as a rule, learn dis-ci-pline, we drill it in.

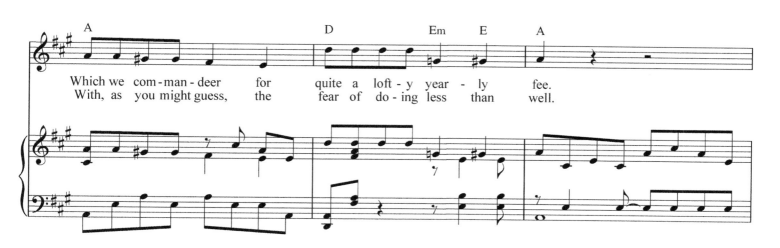

Which we com-man-deer for quite a loft-y year-ly fee.
With, as you might guess, the fear of do-ing less than well.

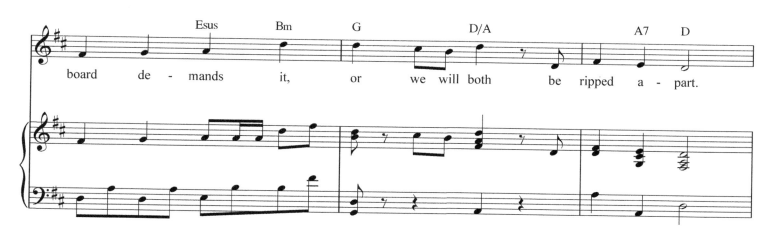

board de - mands it, or we will both be ripped a - part.

D.S. al Coda

There's no in be-tween, we get re - sults here. Or the a-lums will hunt us down.

GOODNIGHT, MY SOMEONE

from Meredith Willson's *The Music Man*

By Meredith Willson

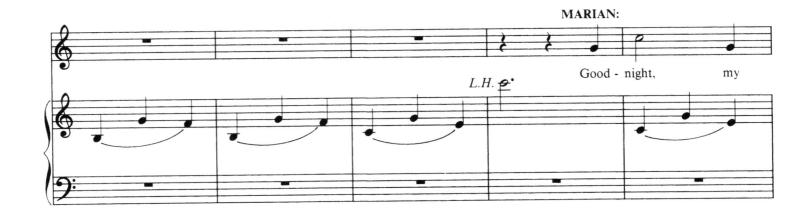

light for good-night, my love, for good-night._____ Sweet

dreams be yours, dear, if dreams there be; Sweet dreams to

car - ry you close to me. I wish they may, and I

wish they might. Now good-night, my some - one, good - night._____

HOME

from Walt Disney's *Beauty and the Beast: The Broadway Musical*

Music by Alan Menken
Lyrics by Tim Rice

BELLE: Yes, I made the choice. For Pa - pa, I will stay.

But I don't de - serve to lose my free - dom in this way, you mon - ster! _____

_____ If you think that what you've done _____ is right, well

HOW LOVELY TO BE A WOMAN

from *Bye Bye Birdie*

Lyric by Lee Adams
Music by Charles Strouse

have that hap - py, grown up, fe - male feel - ing!

How love - ly to be a wom - an! _____ The

wait was well worth - while, _____ how love - ly to

wear mas - ca - ra, _____ and smile a wom - an's

smile. _____ How love - ly to have a fig - ure _____

____ That's round in - stead of flat, _____ When -

ev - er you hear boys whis - tle _____ You're what they're

whis - tling at! It's won-der-ful to feel _____

_____ The way a wom-an feels, _____ It

gives you such a glow Just to know _____ You're

wear - ing lip-stick and heels. _____ How love - ly to

I COULD HAVE DANCED ALL NIGHT

from *My Fair Lady*

Words by Alan Jay Lerner
Music by Frederick Loewe

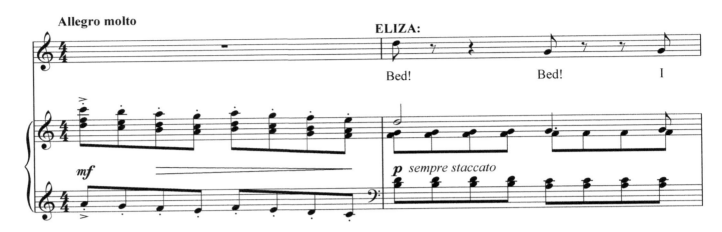

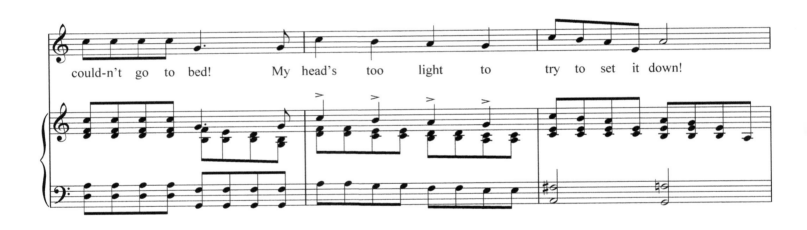

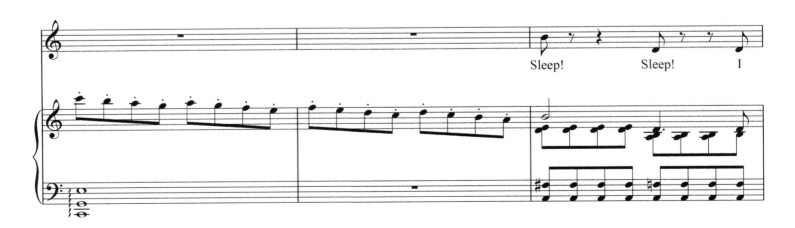

more. I could have spread my wings And done a thou - sand things I've nev - er done be - fore. I'll nev - er know what made it so ex -

L'istesso tempo

night! _____   I could have

danced   all   night! _____ I could have danced   all

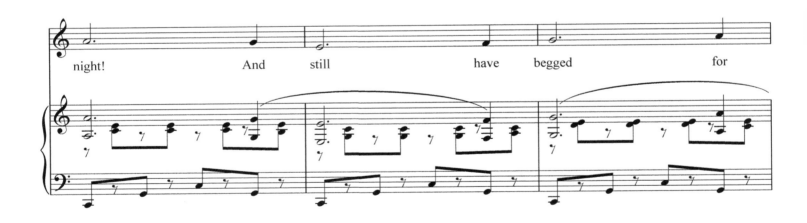

night!   And   still   have   begged   for

more. _____ I could have spread   my

wings _____ And done a thou - sand things I've

nev - er done be - fore. _____

I'll nev - er know _____ what made it so ex -

cit - ing; _____ Why all at once my

I FEEL PRETTY

from *West Side Story*

Lyrics by Stephen Sondheim
Music by Leonard Bernstein

This scene for Maria, Francisca, Rosalia and Consuelo has been adapted as a solo for this edition.

See the pret - ty girl in that mir - ror there: ____ Who can that at -

trac - tive girl be? _____ Such a pret - ty

cresc. *f*

face, Such a pret - ty dress, Such a pret - ty smile, Such a pret - ty me! _____

p sub.

I feel stun - ning ___ And en -

fine, _____ And so pret - ty, _____ Miss A - mer - i - ca can

just re - sign!

See the pret - ty girl in that mir - ror there: _____ Who can that at -

trac - tive girl be? _____ Such a pret - ty face, Such a pret - ty

dress, Such a pret-ty smile, Such a pret-ty me!

I feel stun-ning _ And en-tranc-ing, _ Feel like run-ning and

danc-ing for joy, _____ For I'm loved _____ By a

pret-ty ___ won-der-ful boy! _____

I HAVE DREAMED

from *The King and I*

Lyrics by Oscar Hammerstein II
Music by Richard Rodgers

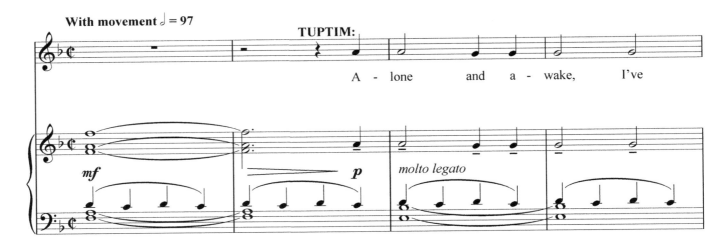

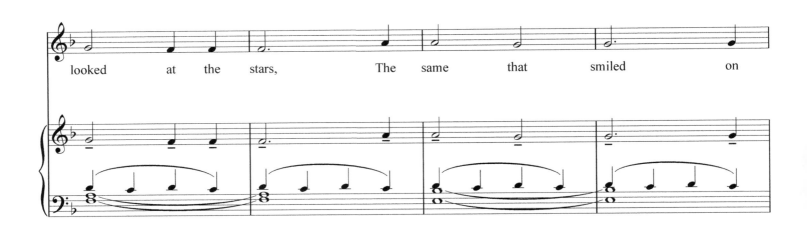

I have dreamed_____ ev - 'ry word you'll

whis - per,_____ When you're close,_____

close to me._____ How you look_____

in the glow of eve - ning,_____

I LOVED YOU ONCE IN SILENCE

from *Camelot*

Words by Alan Jay Lerner
Music by Frederick Loewe

All the while not know - ing_____ You loved me too._____

_____ Yes, loved me_____ in lone - some si - lence;_____

_____ Your heart filled_____ with dark des - pair..._____ Think-ing

love would flame in you for - ev - er, And I'd nev - er,

door._____ Ev - 'ry joy - ous word of love was spo - ken...

poco rit.

rall. Andante

And now there's twice as much grief, Twice the strain for us, Twice the des -

rall.

colla voce

sfz

pair, Twice the pain for us As we had known

be - fore._____

poco rubato

pp

IF I LOVED YOU
from *Carousel*

Lyrics by Oscar Hammerstein II
Music by Richard Rodgers

All I'd want you to know.

If I loved you, Words wouldn't come in an eas - y way.

Round in cir - cles I'd go!

Long - in' to tell you, but a - fraid and shy,

I let my gold-en chan-ces pass me by!

Soon you'd leave me, off___ you would go___ in the mist of day,

Nev - er, nev - er to know___

How I loved you, If I loved you!___

I'LL KNOW
from *Guys And Dolls*

By Frank Loesser

Adapted as a solo here, the song is a duet scene for Sarah and Sky in the show.

love will be just what I need not some fly - by - night Broad - way ro -

mance, and till then I shall wait and till

then _____ I'll be strong _____ for I'll know when my

love _____ comes a - long. _____

IN MY OWN LITTLE CORNER

from *Cinderella*

Lyrics by Oscar Hammerstein II
Music by Richard Rodgers

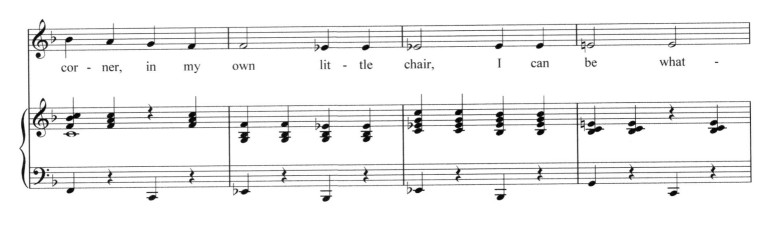

cor - ner, in my own lit - tle chair, I can be what -

ev - er I want to be. _____ On the wing of my

fan - cy I can fly an - y - where And the world will

o - pen its arms to me. _____ I'm a

young Nor - we - gian prin - cess or a milk maid, _____ I'm the

great - est pri - ma don - na in Mi - lan, _____ I'm an

heir - ess who has al - ways had her silk made _____ By her

own flock of silk - worms in Ja - pan! _____ I'm a

girl men go mad for, Love's a game I can play With a

cool and con-fi-dent kind of air, _____ Just as

long as I stay in my own lit-tle cor-ner, _____ All a-

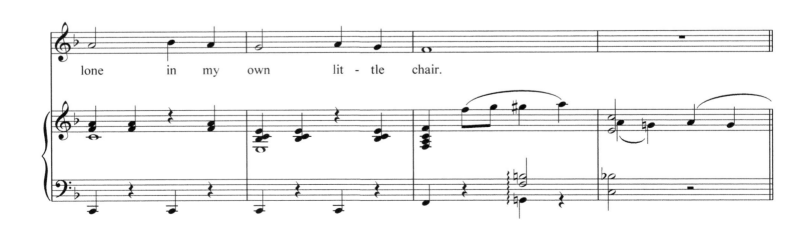

lone in my own lit-tle chair.

I can
be what - ev - er I want to be. _____ I'm a
slave in Cal - cut - ta, I'm a queen in Pe - ru, I'm a
mer - maid danc - ing up - on the sea. _____ I'm a

hunt - ress on an Af - ri - can sa - fa - ri_____ (It's a

dang -'rous type of sport and yet it's fun);_____ In the

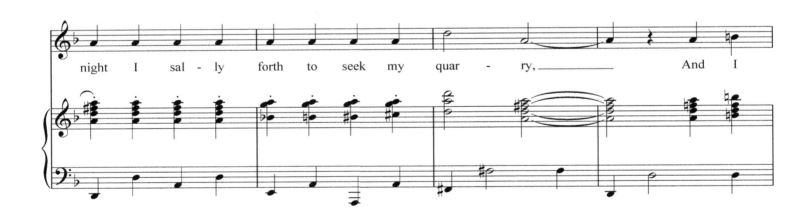

night I sal - ly forth to seek my quar - ry,_____ And I

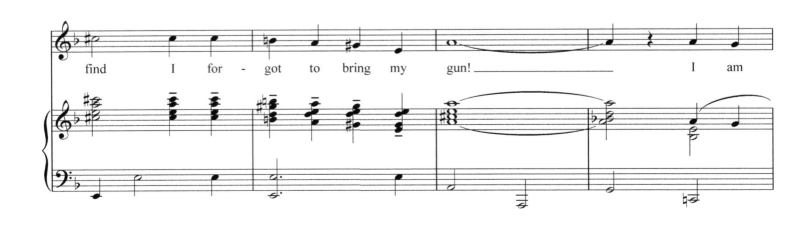

find I for - got to bring my gun!_____ I am

IN MY LIFE

from *Les Misérables*

Music by Claude-Michel Schönberg
Lyrics by Alain Boublil, Jean-Marc Natel
and Herbert Kretzmer

way,___ wait-ing for me.   Does he know I'm a-live?_ Do I know if he's

real?   Does he see___ what I saw?_ Does he feel___ what I

feel?   In my life   I'm no long-er a - lone. Now the love of my life is so

near.   Find me now.   Find me here.

A LITTLE BIT IN LOVE
from *Wonderful Town*

Lyrics by Betty Comden and Adolph Green
Music by Leonard Bernstein

love, ___ then it's love - ly! ___ Mm, _____ It's so

nice to be a - live ___ When you meet some - one _____ who be -

witch - es you. ___ Will he be my all, ___ or did

I just fall a lit - tle bit, ___ a lit - tle bit in

LOVELY
from *A Funny Thing Happened on the Way to the Forum*

Words and Music by
Stephen Sondheim

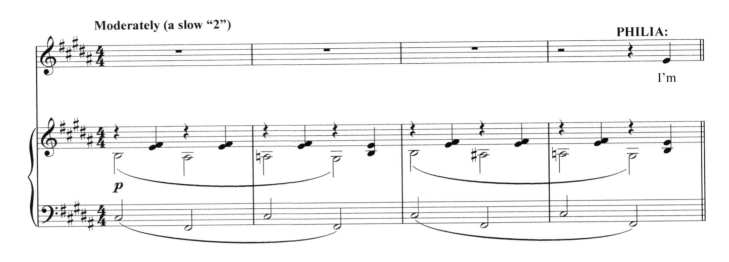

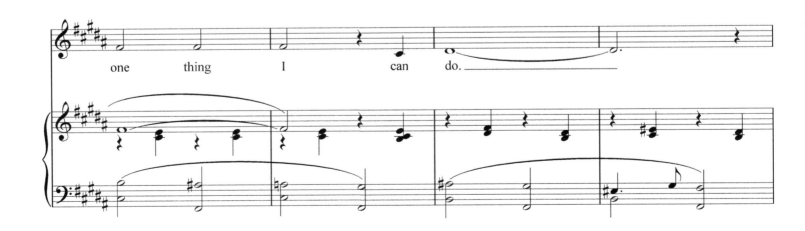

MAKE BELIEVE

from *Show Boat*

Lyrics by Oscar Hammerstein II
Music by Jerome Kern

This song is a duet for Magnolia and Ravenal in the show, adapted as a solo for this edition.

see. And if the things we dream a - bout don't hap - pen__ to be

so,_____ That's_ just an un - im - port - ant tech - ni - cal - i -

Poco animato (♩ = ♪)

ty. Tho' the cold and bru - tal fact is

You and I have nev - er met, We need not

mind con - ven - tion's P's and Q's. _____

If we put our thoughts in prac - tice   We can ban - ish all re -

gret,   I - mag - in - ing most an - y -

thing   we   choose. _____   We could

MANY A NEW DAY

from *Oklahoma!*

Lyrics by Oscar Hammerstein II
Music by Richard Rodgers

LAUREY:

Why should a wo-man who is health - y and strong Blub-ber like a ba-by if her man goes a - way? A - weep-in' and a - wail-in' how he's done her wrong, That's one thing you'll nev - er hear me say! Nev - er gon - na think that the

man I lose is the on-ly man a-mong men. I'll snap my fin-gers to

show I don't care, I'll buy me a brand new dress to wear, I'll scrub my neck and I'll

a tempo

brush my hair And start all o-ver a - gain.

a tempo, con ritmo

Refrain
Con grazia - non legato

Man-y a new face will please my eye, Man-y a new love will find me,

Nev-er-'ve I once looked back to sigh o- ver the ro - mance be - hind me,

Man-y a new day will dawn be - fore I do!

Man-y a light lad may kiss and fly, A kiss gone by is by - gone,

Nev-er-'ve I asked an Au- gust sky, "Where has last Ju - ly gone?"

Nev-er-'ve I wan - dered through the rye, Won-der-in' where has some

guy gone, Man-y a new day will dawn be - fore I do!

Nev-er-'ve I chased the hon - ey bee who care-less-ly ca -

joled me, Some-bod-y else just as sweet as he, cheered me and con -

ON THE STEPS OF THE PALACE

from *Into The Woods*

Words and Music by
Stephen Sondheim

But then what if he knew who you were When you know that you're not what he thinks that he

wants?   And then what if you are _____ What a

prince would en - vi - sion? _____   Al-though how can you know who you are Till you know what you

want, which you don't? So then, which do you pick: Where you're safe out of sight, and your- self, But where ev -'ry-thing's

bet - ter off there where there's noth-ing to choose, so there's noth ing to lose. _____ So you

pry up your shoes. _____ Then from out of the blue, _____

And with - out an - y guide, _____ You know what your de - ci - sion is, _____

Which is not to de - cide. You'll just leave him a clue:

MUCH MORE

from *The Fantasticks*

Words by Tom Jones
Music by Harvey Schmidt

*small notes are optional throughout.

MY FAVORITE THINGS

from *The Sound of Music*

Lyrics by Oscar Hammerstein II
Music by Richard Rodgers

Allegro animato

MARIA:

Rain - drops on ros - es and whis - kers on kit - tens, Bright cop - per

ket - tles and warm wool - en mit - tens, Brown pa - per pack - ag - es

tied up with strings, These are a few of my fa - vor - ite things.

Girls in white dress-es with blue sat-in sash-es, Snow-flakes that
stay on my nose and eye-lash-es, Sil-ver white win-ters that
melt in-to springs, These are a few of my fa-vor-ite things.
When the dog bites, When the bee stings,

When I'm feel - ing sad, _____ I sim - ply re -

mem - ber my fa - vor - ite things and then I don't feel

so bad. _____

MY WHITE KNIGHT
from Meredith Willson's *The Music Man*

Words and Music by
Meredith Willson

self. And more in-t'rest-ed in us than in me. _____

Poco lento

And if oc-ca-sion-'ly he'd pon - der what makes Shake-speare and Bee-thov-en great,

Lento   **Molto lento**

him I could love 'til I die.   Him I could love 'til I die.

Tempo I

My   white   knight, _____ not a Lanc-e-lot ___ nor an an-gel with wings;

Just some-one to love me, _ who is not a-shamed of a few nice things. My white

knight; __ let me walk with him where the oth-ers ride by; Walk, and love him _

Very broadly   **Molto lento**   **Tempo I**

'til I die.   'Til I die. _____

ONCE YOU LOSE YOUR HEART

from *Me and My Girl*

Words and Music by
Noel Gay

Rubato, molto legato, cantabile

Once you lose your heart, Once some-bod-y takes it,

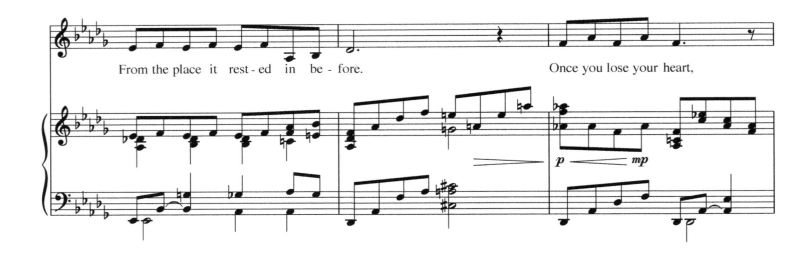

From the place it rest-ed in be - fore. Once you lose your heart,

Once some-bod-y wakes it, then it is - n't your heart an - y more. _____ It's

piu mosso

say a girl should nev - er be with - out love, _____ And

all the joy that love a - lone can bring. All that I have ev - er learnt a -

bout love, _____ tells me it's a ver - y _ fun - ny thing. _____ For

when your heart is fan - cy - free, You hope some man will choose it, But

PART OF YOUR WORLD
from Walt Disney's *The Little Mermaid – A Broadway Musical*

Music by Alan Menken
Lyrics by Howard Ashman

Simply, in 2 (♩ = ca. 76)

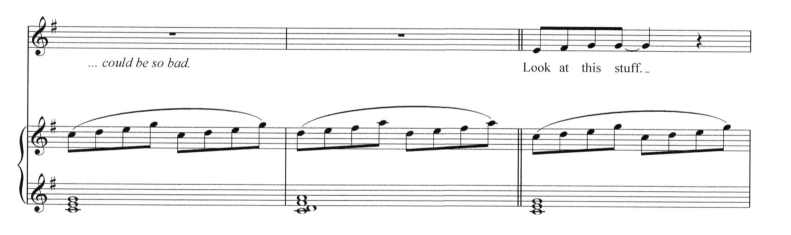

turn? Would - n't I love, love to ex - plore that shore up a -

bove? Out of the sea, wish I could

be part of that world.

OUT OF MY DREAMS

from *Oklahoma!*

Lyrics by Oscar Hammerstein II
Music by Richard Rodgers

Tempo di valse

LAUREY:

Out of my dreams and in-to your arms I long to

fly _____ I will come as eve - ning comes to

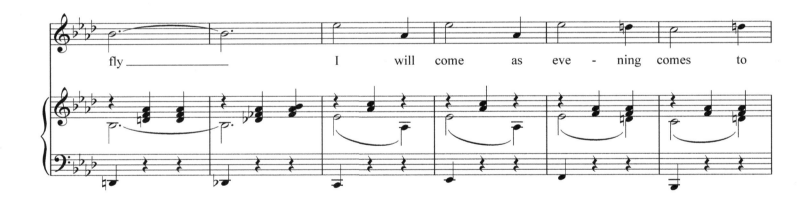

woo a wait - ing sky. _____ Out of my

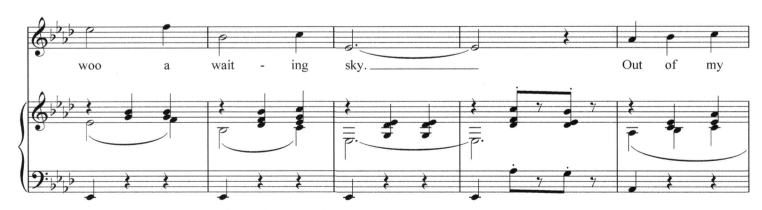

This song appears in a somewhat different form here than in the context of the show.
Mr. Hammerstein revised the lyrics so that the song could stand alone; it is this revision that is used here.

you. _____

Won't have to make up an - y more sto - - - ries

You'll be there! _____ Think of the bright

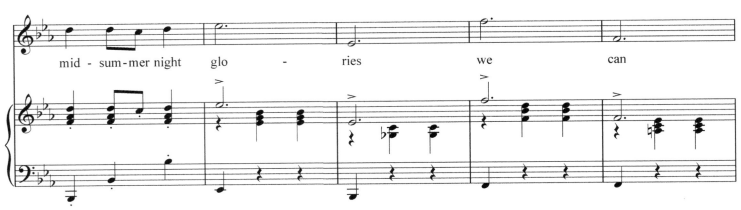

mid - sum-mer night glo - ries we can

152

THE SIMPLE JOYS OF MAIDENHOOD

from *Camelot*

Words by Alan Jay Lerner
Music by Frederick Loewe

Where are the sim-ple joys of maid-en-hood? _____ Where are all those a-dor-ing, dar-ling boys? _____ Where's the knight pin-ing so for me He leaps to death in woe for me? Oh, where are a maid-en's sim-ple joys? _____ Shan't

I have the nor-mal life a maid-en should?_____ Shall I

nev-er be res-cued in the wood?_____ Shall two

knights nev-er tilt for me And let their blood be spilt for me? Oh,

where are the sim-ple joys of maid-en-hood?

Shall I not be on a ped - es - tal, Wor - shipped and com - pet - ed for?

Not be car - ried off, or bet - ter still, Cause a lit - tle war?

poco rall.

a tempo

Where are the sim - ple joys of maid - en - hood? _____ Are those

sweet, gen - tle pleas - ures gone for good? _____ Shall a

feud not be-gin for me? Shall kith not kill their kin for me? Oh,

where are the triv-ial joys...? Harm-less, con-viv-ial joys...?

poco rall.

Where are the sim-ple joys of maid - en -

Poco più mosso

hood?

SIXTEEN GOING ON SEVENTEEN

from *The Sound of Music*

Lyrics by Oscar Hammerstein II
Music by Richard Rodgers

go - ing on sev - en - teen, In - no - cent as a rose.

Bach - e - lor dan - dies, drink - ers of bran - dies, what do I know of

those? To - tal - ly un - pre - pared am I To

face a world of men. Tim - id and shy and

scared am I of things be - yond my ken.

I need some - one old - er and wis - er Tell - ing me what to

do. _____ You are sev - en - teen, go - ing on eight - een,

I'll ____ de - pend ____ on you. _____

SOME THINGS ARE MEANT TO BE

from the Stage Musical *Little Women*

Music by Jason Howland
Lyrics by Mindi Dickstein

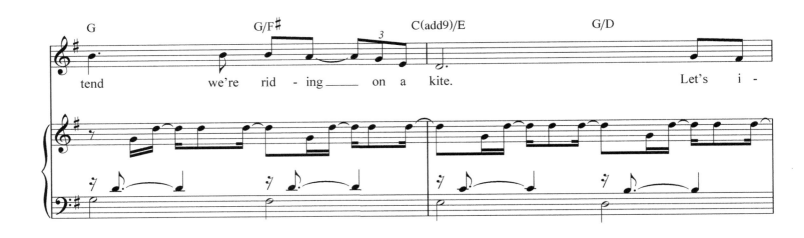

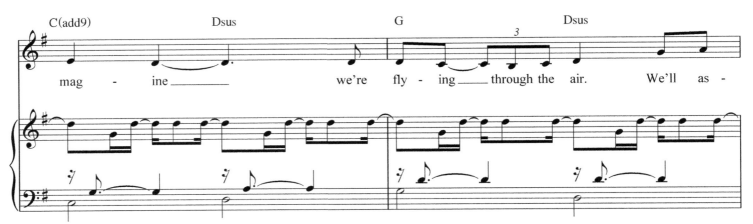

This duet for Beth and Jo is adapted as a solo.

nev - er die: the prom-ise of who you are, your mem-'ries when I am far from

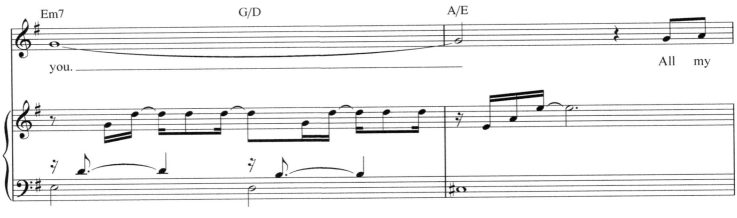

you. _____ All my

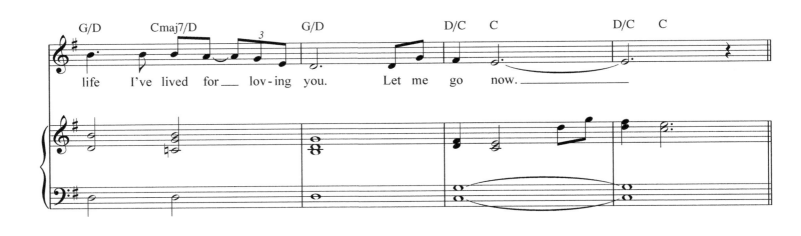

life I've lived for ___ lov-ing you. Let me go now. _____

Tempo I

THE SOUND OF MUSIC

from *The Sound of Music*

Lyrics by Oscar Hammerstein II
Music by Richard Rodgers

I know I will hear what I've heard be-fore. My heart will be blessed with the sound of mu- sic And I'll sing once more.

colla voce

THINK OF ME

from *The Phantom of the Opera*

Music by ANDREW LLOYD WEBBER
Lyrics by CHARLES HART
Additional Lyrics by RICHARD STILGOE

try.

On that day, _____ that not so dis - tant day, _____ when you are

far a - way and free, if you ev - er find a

mo - ment, spare a thought for

me.

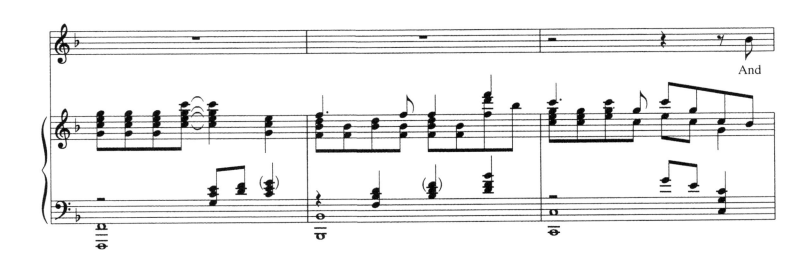

And

though it's clear, though it was al - ways clear _____ that this was nev - er meant to

be, if you hap-pen to re - mem - ber,

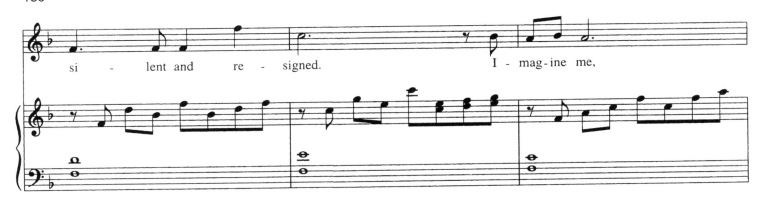

si - lent and re - signed.   I - mag-ine me,

try - ing too hard __ to   put   you from   my   mind.

Think of   me ____ please say you'll think of   me ____ what - ev - er   else   you   choose   to

do.   There   will   nev - er   be   a   day   when

poco più mosso

I won't think of you.

ff

mp

f

Flow-ers fade, ____ the fruits of sum-mer fade, ____ they have their

VANILLA ICE CREAM
from *She Loves Me*

Words by Sheldon Harnick
Music by Jerry Bock

I'm sim - ply stunned! _____ Will won - ders nev - er

cease? Will won - ders nev - er cease? It's been a most pe -

cu - liar day! _____ Will won - ders nev - er

cease? Will won - der nev - er cease? *(Spoken:) Oh!*
Where was I?

TILL THERE WAS YOU

from Meredith Willson's *The Music Man*

By Meredith Willson

There was
love all a-round, but I nev-er heard it sing-ing. No, I
nev-er heard it at all, till there was you.

WE KISS IN A SHADOW

from *The King and I*

Lyrics by Oscar Hammerstein II
Music by Richard Rodgers

This song is a duet for Lun Tha and Tuptin, adapted as a solo for this edition.

To kiss in the sun - light

And say to the sky: Be - hold and be -

lieve what you see! _____ Be - hold how my

rit. *a tempo* *rit.*

lov - er loves me! _____

rit. **pp** *a tempo* *rit.*

WHAT'S THE USE OF WOND'RIN'

from *Carousel*

Lyrics by Oscar Hammerstein II
Music by Richard Rodgers

that. _____ Com-mon sense may tell you, That the

end - in' will be sad, And now's the time to break and run a -

way. But what's the use of won-d'rin' if the end - in' will be sad? He's your

fel - ler and you love him— There's noth-in more to say. _____

Some-thin' made him the way that he is, —

Wheth - er he's false_ or true And some-thin' gave him the

things that are his — One of those things is you. So

when he wants your kiss - es you will give them to the lad, And

WISHING YOU WERE SOMEHOW HERE AGAIN

from *The Phantom of the Opera*

Music by ANDREW LLOYD WEBBER
Lyrics by CHARLES HART
Additional Lyrics by RICHARD STILGOE

WITHOUT YOU

from *My Fair Lady*

Lyrics by Alan Jay Lerner
Music by Frederick Loewe

Allegro con anima

ELIZA:

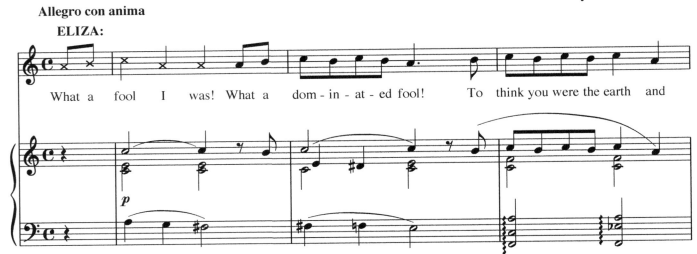

What a fool I was! What a dom-in-at-ed fool! To think you were the earth and

sky. What a fool I was! What an ad-dle-pat-ed fool! What a

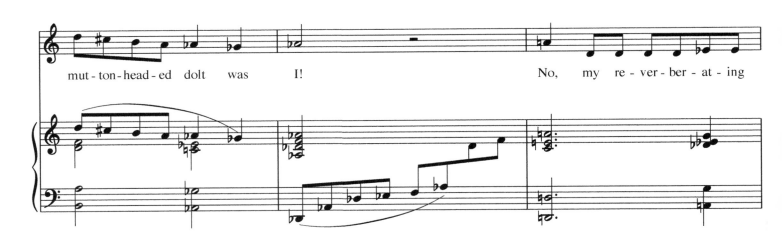

mut-ton-head-ed dolt was I! No, my re-ver-ber-at-ing

friend, You are not the be-gin-ning and the end! _____ There'll be

Allegro con moto

spring ev-'ry year with-out you. Eng-land still will be here with-out

you. There'll be fruit on the tree; and a shore by the sea; there'll be

crum-pets and tea with-out you. Art and mu-sic will thrive with-out

you. Some-how Keats will sur-vive with-out you. And there

still will be rain on that plain down in Spain, e - ven that will re-main with-out

you. I can do _____ with - out

you. You, dear friend, who talk so

WOULDN'T IT BE LOVERLY

from *My Fair Lady*

Words by Alan Jay Lerner
Music by Frederick Loewe

lots of heat; Warm face, warm hands, warm feet, oh, would - n't it be

lov - er - ly? Oh, so lov-er-ly sit - tin' ab - so-bloom - in' -

lute - ly still! I would nev - er budge 'til

Spring crept o - ver me win - der-sill Some - one's head rest - in'

mf dolce